DATE DUE

JUL 1 7 2013			
MAY 2 4 2014			
OCT			
NOV			

W9-CZK-881

HEALTHY
AND HAPPY

Healthy
Bodies

Robyn Hardyman

PowerKiDS
press™
New York

Published in 2012 by The Rosen Publishing Group Inc.
29 East 21st Street, New York, NY 10010

First Edition

Produced for Wayland by Calcium
Design: Paul Myerscough and Geoff Ward
Editor: Sarah Eason
Editor for Wayland: Joyce Bentley
Illustrations: Geoff Ward
Picture Research: Maria Joannou
Consultant: Sue Beck, MSc, BSc

Library of Congress Cataloging-in-Publication Data

Hardyman, Robyn.
Healthy bodies / by Robyn Hardyman. — 1st ed.
    p. cm. — (Healthy and happy)
Includes index.
ISBN 978-1-4488-5274-1 (library binding)
1. Exercise—Juvenile literature. 2. Health—Juvenile literature. I. Title. II. Series.
RA781.H35 2012
613.7'1—dc22

                          2010046294

Photographs: Dreamstime: Galina Barskaya 17; Istockphoto: Wouter van Caspel 12, Vlad Turchenko 1, 22; Shutterstock: Matt Antonino 4, Cheryl Casey 24, Jacek Chabraszewski 5, Jaimie Duplass 14, Sonya Etchison 16, Gelpi 2, 21, GeoM 26, Goldenangel 13, Inc 7, Kruchankova Maya 18, Monkey Business Images 8, 11, 27, Paulaphoto 23, Govorov Pavel 19, Matt Ragen 25, Dmitriy Shironosov 9, Lorraine Swanson 20, Leah-Anne Thompson 10, Zdorov Kirill Vladimirovich 15, Clive Watkins 6.

Cover photograph: Shutterstock/Jaimie Duplass

Manufactured in China
CPSIA Compliance Information: Batch # WAS1102PK: For Further Information contact Rosen Publishing, New York, New York at 1-800-237-9932

Contents

Exercise and Play Every Day

Exercise and play help to keep you healthy. Doing something active, such as playing a chasing game, uses your body and makes it work better. When you feel healthy, you are more likely to feel happy.

Playing tennis is healthy and a great way to keep fit.

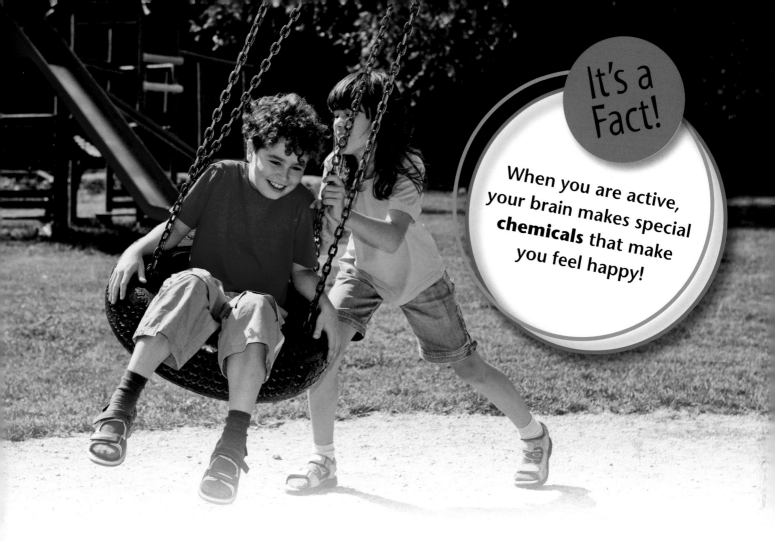

Being Active

There are many different ways to be active. You can swim, play football, or just run around with your friends. The more active you are, the healthier and fitter you will be.

Enjoying yourself outside often means you are being active without knowing it.

Playing Outside

Play outside as much as you can—there is more room to run around and make noise. Fresh air is also good for your **lungs** and your whole body.

What Is Exercise?

Exercise is any activity that makes you move your arms and legs more than usual. When you exercise hard, you exercise your lungs and **heart,** too. Exercise also makes your brain work better.

Playing in a team can help you to make new friends.

It's a Fact!

An active child walks more than 10,000 steps every day!

Everyday Exercise

Many things you do every day involve exercise.
You are being active when you walk to school.
See if you can be more active when you are out.
Try using the stairs instead of taking the elevator.

Favorite Activities

You probably enjoy some
activities more than others.
Which are your favorites
on this list?

- swimming
- football
- dancing
- playing chase
- gymnastics
- running
- walking
- cycling
- climbing
- judo

*Get your family to exercise,
too! You could go on a
bicycle ride together.*

What Is Play?

Playing is all about having fun. When you play, you relax—and that helps to keep you happy and healthy. You can play on your own or with others.

Quiet and Active

Play can be energetic, such as splashing in a swimming pool. It can also be less active, such as playing marbles.

Playing a clapping game helps you to think and react quickly.

8

Here are some ideas for playtime—do you do any of these?

At Home
- practice handstands and cartwheels
- dance to your favorite music
- practice dribbling a basketball.

You can improve your balance by practicing handstands.

At School
- play tag
- practice scoring goals
- climb on the jungle gym.

HEALTHY HINTS

Improve your ball skills playing "keep it up." You can use any part of your body except your hands to keep a ball in the air.

Let's Pretend!

Pretend games are a good way to exercise your brain. You can play games that use your imagination, such as pretending to be a favorite book or television character.

Dressing Up

Make a dress up trunk by asking your family for old clothes, hats, and jewelry. You could make up you own story, then dress up to act it out.

Dress up as a pirate and pretend to sail the high seas in search of treasure!

Writing, Drawing, and Music

If you are on your own, try writing a story or drawing a picture. You could also practice singing or playing a musical instrument.

You can create your own imaginary stories when you play with your toys.

Get Ready, Get Set, Go!

You have to get ready for some kinds of exercise. If you are going to do something very energetic, warm up your body first. This will help you to exercise safely.

HEALTHY HINTS

Try these exercises to warm up your body. Bend and stretch your arms. Bend a knee, and hold your foot against your bottom. Do the same on the other leg. Touch your toes.

Stretching gets you ready for exercise.

A helmet and pads will protect your head and body if you fall while you are skateboarding.

Starting Slowly

Start gently when you exercise so you do not hurt yourself. You can go faster little by little!

Sports Clothes

Exercising is more comfortable in loose clothes and shoes such as sneakers. Don't forget to wear protective pads and a helmet if you are cycling, skateboarding, or rollerblading.

Muscles and Joints

You use your **muscles** and **joints** to move your body. Your muscles are the soft flesh you can feel under your skin.

Moving Bones

Muscles are attached to your bones. When you tighten a muscle, it becomes shorter. This pulls on the bone to make it move.

It's a Fact!

The biggest muscles are the ones in your bottom.

Your elbows are the joints that allow you to bend your arms.

Bend Your Body

A joint is where two bones meet. For example, your knee is the joint where your leg bones meet. You can only bend or move your bones at a joint.

You bend and straighten your legs and arms when you play on a swing.

Healthy Heart and Lungs

When you exercise, your lungs pump a gas called **oxygen** into your blood. Your heart pumps this blood around your body.

Making Energy

Blood contains sugar from the food you eat and oxygen from the air you breathe. Muscles change the sugar and oxygen into **energy**.

You can feel your heart beating strongly when you stop after a race.

Keeping Healthy

The more you exercise, the healthier your heart and lungs will be. When your heart and lungs are healthy, you can do more before you get out of breath.

You need to rest for a minute or two to catch your breath after you have been running.

It's a Fact!

Your lungs can take in ten times more air when you exercise than when you do not.

17

Run, Jump, and Throw

Different kinds of exercise make your body fit and healthy in different ways. Running and jumping exercise your heart and lungs. They also make your leg muscles stronger.

Skipping

Many top athletes exercise by using a jump rope. Jumping rope involves skipping over the rope in place.

It is great to learn a new skill, such as jumping rope. You will get better as you practice.

Ball Games

Throwing a ball uses the muscles in your arms, chest, and shoulders. Catching or kicking a ball helps your eyes and muscles work together.

You have to control your leg muscles when you dribble a ball.

HEALTHY HINTS

Have a throwing competition with your friends. The person who throws a tennis ball the farthest wins a reward badge (see pages 28–29).

Climb, Stretch, and Balance

Many kinds of exercise keep your joints **flexible**, or bendy. Climbing uses all your muscles and joints as you stretch, pull, and push.

You could learn how to ice skate and improve your balance playing hockey.

HEALTHY HINTS

Stop exercising immediately if you feel dizzy, pain, or find it difficult to breathe. Tell an adult what has happened.

Ballet, Judo, and Gymnastics

Ballet, gymnastics, and judo are good ways to stretch your joints and make them stronger.

Balancing Act

Some simple exercises can help to improve your balance. Can you walk along a line on the ground? How long can you stand on one leg without holding onto anything?

Jumping around and dancing to music help to keep your joints flexible.

Swim and Splash

Swimming exercises all the muscles in your body. Your legs, arms, back, and stomach all work hard to make you swim through the water. Swimming also exercises your heart and lungs.

Remember to hold your breath when your face is under the water!

Swimming Strokes

There are four swimming strokes—freestyle, backstroke, breaststroke, and butterfly. Each stroke exercises different muscles in your body.

HEALTHY HINTS

Remember to only swim when there is an adult with you. Stay in a depth of water that is safe for you.

Playing in the Pool

It's a lot of fun playing games with your friends in the pool, such as tag. As you become a better swimmer, you can learn how to dive, too. Good swimmers can learn other water sports, such as water aerobics and water polo.

It's fun to play with inflatable toys in the swimming pool.

Keep Cool

Exercise makes you hot, so your body needs to cool down. When you exercise, more blood is pumped close to the surface of your skin. The blood then cools down, and this helps to cool down your body.

You can look flushed or red when your blood pumps to the surface of your skin during exercise.

HEALTHY HINTS

When you stop exercising, you start to cool down. Put on some warm clothes after exercising, so you don't cool down too quickly.

Sweating

When you exercise, you sweat. Sweat is salty liquid. It escapes from your body through tiny holes in your skin called **pores**. The sweat soon dries on your skin. As it dries, it cools your skin.

Drinking Water

Exercise makes you thirsty. You should drink lots of water when you exercise to replace the water you lose when you sweat.

Drinking water during and after exercise will give you more energy.

Using Up Energy

When you exercise, your body uses energy from the food you eat. This stops you becoming overweight. But if you eat more food than you need, your body stores it as fat and you put on weight. It is unhealthy to weigh too much.

Watching television is a good way to relax, but make sure you do plenty of exercise, too.

Feeling Good

Do something active at playtime. Exercise releases chemicals that make you feel happier and calmer. This will make it easier to work in class. Joining in activities helps you to make friends, too.

Relaxing and Sleeping

Being active helps you to relax. If you do plenty of exercise during the day, you will sleep better at night. So, keep exercising, keep healthy, and keep happy!

Sleep allows your body and mind to rest and recover, ready for another active day.

HEALTHY HINTS

Don't be a "couch potato"! Try to exercise for at least an hour every day.

Make Reward Badges

Make reward badges for you and your friends. You could hold your own sports day and use the badges for prizes.

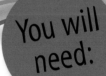
1. Use the egg cup to draw circles on a large sheet of card. Draw the circles close together to fit in as many as possible.

2. Cut out the circles.

3. Draw smiley faces and other designs on the badges. Use gold stars and pens to make the badges colorful. Or you could color them in gold, silver, and bronze to look like medals.

4. Cut a strip of double-sided tape a little bit shorter than the widest part of the circle.

5. Stick the tape to the back of a badge.

6. When you are ready to award a badge, peel the protective paper off the tape and stick the badge on your friend's clothing. Well done!

Make some more badges when you run out. Exercise is for life!

Exercise Topic Web

Use this topic web to discover themes and ideas in subjects that are related to exercise.

HEALTH EDUCATION
- How to make exercise sociable by playing and exercising with friends.
- How to make exercise a family event.
- How exercise can aid relaxation and reduce stress.

ART AND DESIGN
- How to make reward badges using junk material.
- Imaginative play through drawing.

LITERATURE & DRAMA
- Write a play or a story that includes characters, then act it out.

EXERCISE

MUSIC
- How music and songwriting can be used in imaginative play.
- Write a song and sing it aloud.

SCIENCE
- The health benefits of exercise, including improved fitness, flexibility, muscle strength.
- How exercise helps people to maintain a healthy weight.
- How exercise helps to bring about a sense of wellbeing.
- An understanding of how the components of the body work: heart, lungs, muscles, bones, and joints.
- The importance of keeping the body hydrated.

PE
- How different types of sports and activities are all forms of exercise, from cycling and running to tennis, ice skating, and rollerblading.

Glossary

chemicals substances in the body that affect how it behaves

energy being able to do physical things

flexible being able to bend easily

heart a muscular organ that pumps blood around the body

joints places where two or more bones meet

judo a Japanese sport that involves kicking and wrestling

lungs organs used to breathe in oxygen from the air

muscles flesh that contracts and relaxes to move your bones

oxygen one of the gases in the air

pores tiny holes in your skin through which sweat passes

Further Information and Web Sites

Books

Being Healthy, Feeling Great: Exercise
by Robyn Hardyman
(PowerKids Press, 2010)

Healthy Choices: Exercise and Play
by Cath Senker
(PowerKids Press, 2008)

Looking After Me: Exercise
by Liz Gogerly
(Crabtree Publishing, 2008)

Web Sites

Due to the changing nature of Internet links, PowerKids Press has developed an online list of Web sites related to the subject of this book. This site is updated regularly. Please use this link to access this list:
www.powerkidslinks.com/hah/bodies/

Index